CREDIT & SAVINGS
FOR DEVELOPMENT

**by Stephen Devereux and Henry Pares,
with John Best**

Series editor: Brian Pratt

Revised 1989 by Brian Pratt

British Library Cataloguing in Publication Data
Devereux, Stephen
    Credit and savings for development. – 2nd ed.
    1. Developing countries. Personal income
    I. Title II. Pares, Henry III. Best, John 1943–
    IV. Devereux, Stephen. Manual of credit and savings for the poor of
    developing countries
    322.0240091724

    ISBN 0-85598-159-8
    ISBN 0-85598-160-1 pbk

Published by Oxfam
274 Banbury Road
Oxford OX2 7DZ
United Kingdom

Produced by Oxfam Design Studio
Printed by Oxfam Print Unit

Contents

Index of Case Studies

Acknowledgments

Thanks to Steve Duke, Tony Hammond, Roger King, Rachel Percy Ogunlola, Betty Wilkinson and Simon Collings for help in the production of the first edition of this Manual.

Thanks also to Trevor Bottomley, Patrick Sweeting, Mira Savara and James Copestake for comments and additional material for this revised edition.

Introduction

The very poor in developing countries commonly lack funds to increase production and improve their living standards. This short book seeks to introduce readers to one way round this obstacle: small-scale credit. It discusses constraints on the provision of credit and social factors which affect its availability and use. It is hoped that it will be of practical help to development workers who plan, implement and evaluate projects involving savings and credit schemes for the very poor.

The book focuses mainly on the savings and credit needs of the rural poor, but many of the points made are equally applicable to those in the urban informal economy; indeed several examples are drawn from this field. (A companion volume on income generation in poor urban areas will be published in 1990.) It is in two main parts. Part One consists of two chapters. The first analyses the rural household economy and the situations in which credit needs arise. The second chapter outlines the types, disadvantages and advantages of rural financial institutions. This leads on to the major part of the book, Part Two, which discusses problems experienced in implementing development schemes to mobilise credit and savings resources.

These problems are grouped under several chapter headings, illustrated by examples, mostly from projects supported by Oxfam. The first chapter, on access to credit, looks at the problems of would-be borrowers, but the next two, on creditworthiness and default, deal with these factors from the lenders' point of view. Methods of saving follow, being at least as important for self-sufficient community development as credit schemes, and after savings come issues associated with project design and participation. The discussion concludes with a warning of credit's tendency to create new dependencies.

A Conclusion, containing policy guidelines, completes the book. There is an Appendix which outlines how to identify rural financial needs and the scope for intervention through a process of participatory research. Checklists of questions which can be used are included, and also a flowchart of a set of decision guidelines.

NOTE
Writings on rural credit unfortunately tend to reflect the priorities and prejudices of lenders and assume that the financial decision-maker is invariably male. Wherever appropriate this book tries to avoid this pitfall and uses pronouns of indefinite sex. This has not been possible, however, when quoting from other authors.

PART ONE

AN APPROACH TO RURAL CREDIT AND SAVINGS

Chapter 1

THE RURAL ECONOMY

1.1 The household economy

Rural households in developing countries are not like the family 'farm firms' of Western European or American agriculture – businesses which produce goods for cash profit. Some of the key objectives of these households have little to do with profit making, and do not lend themselves to analysis in terms of simple profit and loss. They are:

- Year-to-year survival by means of a farming system which has been shown to give a reasonably secure food supply.
- Meeting needs for a wide range of goods and services other than food – housing, clothing, tools, utensils, medicine, school fees.
- Performing a social role, which involves a complex of rights and obligations and varies between households according to their social and economic status.
- Increasing, where possible, the household's wealth and status in the community through buying land and other assets.
- Improving the living standards of the household members.

It is important to realise that in order to achieve these objectives most households carry out a wide range of economic activities other than the production of crops and livestock. These activities are often ignored by planners of rural development programmes because they are not agricultural, or are not carried out by the household head, or because the products are only used in the home. These time-consuming activities include:

- transporting and marketing produce
- processing and storing produce
- collecting water and firewood
- building and repairing homes
- making household goods (mats, utensils, etc.)
- making/repairing implements for use in productive activities
- child care.

3

In many communities some members may be engaged in various other activities, among them hunting, gathering, fishing, making goods for sale, providing services for sale, trading and wage employment.

Just as the household has many activities besides agricultural production, so there are many demands on cash, including that which becomes available through credit, for purposes other than agricultural investment. In fact such investment may not be a particularly high priority for a poor household.

The household economy can be thought of as a tree, drawing up water through its roots in order to feed its branches; the water represents money, the roots the various sources from which it can be obtained, and the branches the competing demands for any cash which enters the household (see Figure 1).

The lower branches, representing basic needs and rents and taxes, must be given priority, since until they are satisfied other expenditure decisions cannot be considered. Once these basic needs have been met, there are other pressing calls on household funds. Social obligations may entail expenditure on ceremonies, entertainment and gifts which is not only obligatory but regarded as an investment.

Education is another form of investment which is perceived as less risky than investment in agriculture but its benefits are realised only in the long term, so it often receives lower priority than the more urgent need to increase agricultural output. Nevertheless, agricultural investment is represented by the tree's higher branches because funds tend to be allocated to it only when the needs represented by lower branches have been satisfied. Similarly, only if any funds remain after these essential expenses have been met does investment in education, lending or savings take place.

With regard to credit, the 'household economy tree' demonstrates two very important and related points:

1. Productive investment in agriculture is a much lower priority for a poor small farmer than it is for a larger and wealthier one – yet 'productive investment in agriculture' is usually the only purpose for which banks will provide loans to farmers. If productive investment becomes more attractive because of, say, higher crop prices, the demand for such credit rises. But the tree shows that there is no single link from any one root to any one branch, so that any credit given to a household affects every aspect of its economic situation and behaviour.

4

Figure 1. The Household Economy as a Tree.

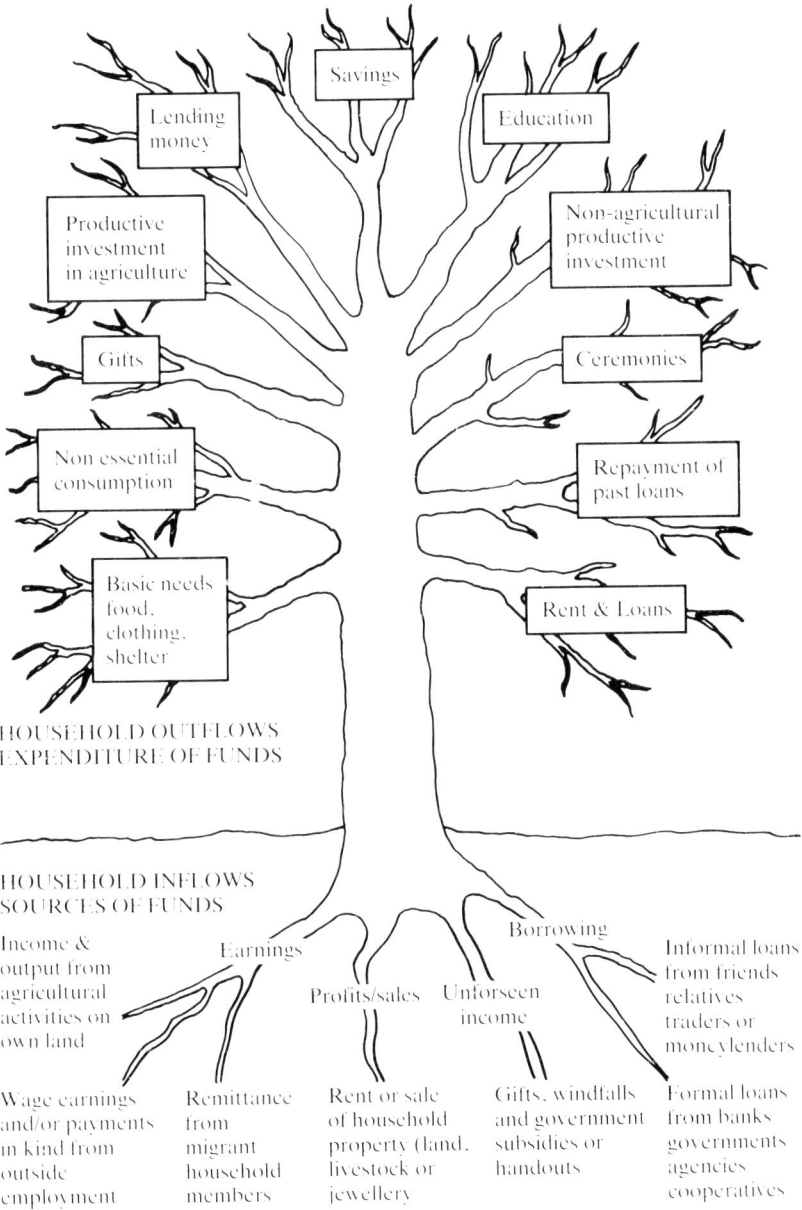

Savings

Lending money

Education

Productive investment in agriculture

Non-agricultural productive investment

Gifts

Ceremonies

Non essential consumption

Repayment of past loans

Basic needs food, clothing, shelter

Rent & Loans

HOUSEHOLD OUTFLOWS
EXPENDITURE OF FUNDS

HOUSEHOLD INFLOWS
SOURCES OF FUNDS

Income & output from agricultural activities on own land

Earnings

Borrowing

Informal loans from friends relatives traders or moneylenders

Profits/sales

Unforseen income

Wage earnings and/or payments in kind from outside employment

Remittance from migrant household members

Rent or sale of household property (land, livestock or jewellery

Gifts, windfalls and government subsidies or handouts

Formal loans from banks governments agencies cooperatives

5

2. Distinctions between 'consumption' and 'production' credit, or between 'agricultural' and 'non-agricultural' credit, are often meaningless in practice. Where money is needed urgently for a particular purpose (medicine, debt repayments or taxes, for example), then incoming funds will be used for that purpose first, whether it is agricultural or not. In other words, a lender cannot ensure that any loan will be used for a particular purpose unless that purpose also accords with the borrower's own priorities, although attempts to enforce its use for a specific purpose may well be made.

1.2 Needs for credit

If a household wants or needs to make expenditures which are, within any period of time, larger than its income for the same period, then it will need either:
- to draw upon its **savings** or
- to make use of **credit.**

There are two reasons for such expenditures:

1. Unusually low income, caused, for example, by a poor harvest or perhaps an illness which stops a key member of the household working.

2. Unusually high expenditure for both planned and unforeseen purposes. Planned purposes include religious festivals, marriages, taxes, school fees, seed, fertiliser or extra labour at peak periods of the agricultural year, and investment in costly productive resources (a plough or an irrigation pump, for example). Unforeseen or unplanned purposes include family emergencies such as illness or death and recovery and rehabilitation after a natural disaster.

In a credit and savings programme, as with any development programme, it is important to have a clear picture of the household, as well as the economic and social structures affecting it. The poor are part of a wider context which needs to be understood if a programme is to target them successfully and have a positive impact on their lives.

Chapter 2

RURAL FINANCIAL INSTITUTIONS

In order to save or to obtain credit, a household will first make use of the most readily available methods. Virtually all societies have established their own arrangements for saving and credit and it is to these that an individual or household is likely to turn first; they are termed 'informal' institutions. If an individual goes beyond the village and uses, say, a co-operative society, a post office or a bank, either to deposit money or as the source of a loan, s/he is said to have access to 'formal' institutions.

Informal and formal institutions can be distinguished from one another in a variety of ways. In informal savings and credit systems, a lender, who may be a borrower's friend or landlord or else a professional moneylender, makes loans on their own account and bears the full risk of default personally. Formal institutions, by contrast, act as intermediaries between those from whom they take deposits and those to whom they give loans, reconciling the interests of savers and borrowers who may be far removed from each other. They are specifically designed for credit and savings, and operate in the banking/finance sector of the economy (whether for profit or not).

Simple person-to-person arrangements, based on personal knowledge of each other's affairs and without written agreements, are usually considered adequate in informal systems. Formal institutions, on the other hand, operate a set of procedures designed to reduce the need for close personal supervision of their clients. Subjective assessment of the ability to repay a loan is replaced by judgement against a set of criteria by which creditworthiness is assessed (form and size of land holding, for example), and is supported by pledges of security in the form of land or other assets. In practice this means that formal institutions tend to lend only to those who already have assets, not to the very poor.

2.1 Informal savings and credit

Several methods of informal saving are traditionally open to rural households, including the following:

- hoarding money, or buying gold, jewellery and other valuables
- holdings of livestock or stores of commodities such as grain
- depositing money with a trusted individual
- rotating savings groups, in which each member deposits a small amount of money regularly into a central fund, the whole of which is given to each member in turn, perhaps by drawing lots.

There are, however, disadvantages to saving by these means:

- They rarely earn interest.
- Inflation causes cash savings to fall in value (though savings in the form of physical assets may retain their purchasing power).
- Making deposits and withdrawals can be inconvenient, and there may be few incentives to make regular deposits.
- There are risks involved – theft of money or valuables, death of animals, deterioration of stored commodities, and embezzlement.
- Many savings groups are designed to meet consumption, not investment, needs.

However, informal methods of saving play an important, often indispensable role in developing countries, especially where credit is difficult or expensive to come by.

Informal credit is available from several sorts of lender:

- owners of capital assets (rickshaws, buses, small irrigation pumps, etc.)
- relatives and friends with whom reciprocal arrangements are often made
- shopkeepers or other suppliers
- produce buyers
- moneylenders
- landlords
- other wealthy individuals.

There are, however, significant problems with these sources of credit:

1. Borrowers may become involved in obligations to lenders which, strictly speaking, have nothing to do with their loans; they may be obliged to perform services, make presents or provide political support. They may find themselves inhibited from opposing the lender in village meetings, or dissuaded from joining co-operatives or

other social action groups of which the lender disapproves. On the other hand, personal conflicts can prevent a successful person from getting credit.

2. Lenders may insist that borrowers buy their supplies from them or sell their produce to them; further, they may impose unfair prices on borrowers and prevent them from buying and selling at normal market rates.

3. Even allowing for the risks inherent in lending without security, interest rates may still be excessively high. Lenders may use high priced credit to gain permanent economic power over borrowers, forcing them and their families into a state of perpetual indebtedness so as to command control of their labour. In extreme cases they may even bond successive generations of an indebted family to their service.

4. Lenders may deliberately insist on repayment of loans at awkward times, obliging borrowers to make 'distress sales' of land and other productive assets to them for less than their market value.

5. There are no flows of internal funds between areas, so cash-poor areas cannot get funds from cash-rich areas, nor will interest rates equalise across regions.

The more unequal the relationship between a lender and a borrower, the more severe these disadvantages can become. Where lenders are seeking to establish themselves in the position of power which lending money can confer, they may even use physical violence, or the threat of it, to prevent borrowers from defaulting, to seize property from defaulters, or to enforce additional obligations of service, labour or trade upon them.

These are the worst aspects of informal credit. It is important to take a balanced view. A good deal of informal lending and borrowing takes place between individuals of similar status (a common example being the rotating savings group), and even where a moneylender, trader or landlord does lend to a small farmer or artisan, he does not necessarily seek to exploit the borrower's relative weakness. A landlord who receives some of his tenants' produce as rent may even extend loans for investment purposes to his tenant at subsidised interest rates, since increased production is to their mutual advantage.

The most serious disadvantage of informal credit is its inadequate

When an informal credit system goes wrong it can be disastrous for the
borrower. Tejiabhai Bilwal borrowed Rs 1,100 from a moneylender
against silver ornaments worth Rs 12,500. Although he paid back Rs
2,300, the ornaments were not returned. Now the moneylender is
denying the repayment was made and is demanding Rs 7,000.

scope. Most lenders are only prepared to give short-term loans, for a single crop season in the case of farmers or, in the case of handicraft producers, for a single production cycle from raw material purchase to sale of finished products. There are few informal lenders who will finance the purchase of capital assets and allow the repayments to be spread over several years. Furthermore, informal lenders usually finance traditional rather than innovative activities.

Nevertheless, the continued use of informal savings and credit mechanisms is a proof of their usefulness. Their main advantage is accessibility. In contrast to formal credit schemes, informal borrowing requires neither literacy, nor costly and time-consuming journeys away from the village, nor adherence to specific office opening hours. Transactions are mostly carried out with familiar faces in familiar surroundings.

In addition to these general advantages of simplicity and convenience, informal borrowing has the specific advantage of not requiring formal security; rather, it is based on lenders' understanding of specific borrowers' needs and their likely ability to repay. Loans can be monitored in the normal course of village life. These advantages are further covered in Sections 3.2 and 3.3.

In practice, informal credit plays a crucial role for the many people who cannot obtain formal credit.

2.2 Formal financial institutions

In principle, formal institutions for savings and credit are in a position to meet needs that the informal sector cannot. For savers, a bank or post office may provide the means to make small deposits in a secure place where they can earn interest. For borrowers, formal institutions can channel funds, including funds from other areas, to the rural sector at more reasonable interest rates and for longer periods than informal lenders.

In practice, however, the performance of formal institutions leaves much to be desired. The main problem is that certain groups of rural borrowers, especially small farmers, tenants and landless labourers, find it difficult to gain access to funds from such institutions, while large farmers, whose need for credit is usually less urgent, enjoy ready access to them.

Two main types of formal institution operate in the rural economy:
– **commercial banks**
– specialist farm credit institutions (or SFCIs), usually established by

governments, which go by a variety of names, e.g. Agricultural Development Bank, Agricultural Finance Corporation, Rural Development Bank, etc.

Commercial Banks

Commercial banks establish operations in rural areas firstly to obtain deposits by encouraging the opening of savings accounts and secondly to make loans where they can find sufficiently creditworthy borrowers. While people in rural areas, however, may find banks attractive for their savings, the criteria banks apply for lending prevent most small farmers, traders and artisans from obtaining loans from them. Two conclusions may be drawn:

1. Most commercial banks are unwilling to extend credit to rural people who have few suitable assets to offer as security or collateral.

2. The alleged lack of creditworthy rural borrowers results in savings deposits being channelled from rural to urban areas.

Specialist Farm Credit Institutions

SFCIs are set up in response to the perceived failure of commercial banks to serve farmers adequately. Their operations tend to be based on two assumptions. Firstly, that farmers who are poor have little capacity for saving, so that if innovation is to occur it must be financed by credit. Secondly, that innovation generally promotes the welfare of poor rural people and can be stimulated if credit is made available on favourable terms. As a result most SFCIs have the following features:

– They engage only in lending, not in deposit taking.

– They operate with limited amounts of public funds.

– They are required to lend at concessionary interest rates, which increases their bias against poor, 'uncreditworthy' borrowers.

– Instead of a demand for collateral security, they may insist on strict conditions on the use to which loans are put. Loans tend to be given for specified investment and often take the form of a package of innovative inputs calculated, after taking repayments into account, to increase a borrower's income.

In contrast to commercial banks, which often have surprisingly little effect on rural financial markets, SFCIs succeed in making an impact which is both significant and often, unfortunately, negative. In concentrating exclusively on the provision of credit, SFCIs make no contribution to the mobilisation of rural savings. Indeed, the provision of credit on favourable terms may even discourage informal institutions like rotating savings groups.

Since their funds are provided by government, not the financial market, SFCIs may have difficulty in assessing the real nature of the market in which they operate, and become alienated from their borrowers, who tend to see them as institutions to be exploited ("government's money is everybody's money").

The criteria by which funds are allocated may be politically biased or even arbitrary. If political criteria are employed, funds are loaned to those who exert sufficient influence, pay the necessary bribes or require appeasement by government. If there is arbitrary selection of borrowers, in order to meet disbursement quotas for example, the result may be that small farmers are handed disproportionately large sums of money and required to adopt innovation on a scale beyond their managerial or risk-bearing capacity. Both of these situations represent inefficient allocation of funds and the latter carries the risk that borrowers may find themselves saddled with repayment commitments which they cannot meet – a situation more commonly found with certain types of informal moneylending.

It appears, by and large, that existing formal institutions do not serve the rural poor effectively, partly because they fail to identify the real needs and partly because their structures and objectives prevent them from making a flexible response to these needs. In Part 2 Oxfam's many experiences of credit programmes are drawn upon to review some of the key issues and problems associated with their implementation.

Village seed-banks and grain stores can be an effective way of assisting subsistence farmers. Workers and officials inspect millet from a village grain store in Burkina Faso.

PART TWO

ISSUES RAISED IN THE IMPLEMENTATION OF CREDIT AND SAVINGS PROGRAMMES

Chapter 3

ACCESS TO CREDIT

3.1 Remoteness from the cash economy

Credit schemes rely heavily on participants having ready access to markets for their goods. For this reason credit and marketing schemes often go together. Without assured outlets for the sale of their produce, small and marginal farmers would be ill-advised to use credit for any inputs required to raise productivity.

The marginal farmer's first priority is to produce enough to feed the family; a surplus to sell comes second. Until a farmer gains access to the market the most appropriate loan may be in kind – seed, fertiliser and possibly implements – with harvest-time repayment also in kind. One way of achieving this is to establish a revolving seed bank, perhaps linked to a village grain store.

> **In Gujarat, Oxfam has supported and set up village seed banks for the very poor. These are administered by local people. They make local seed available in the planting season and are repaid the same amount of seed grain, plus 25% extra as interest, at harvest-time. The seed banks have proved popular and successful, with 100% repayment rates, and are also acting as institution-builders at local village level.**

Without access to the cash economy the means of repaying a loan for a capital project are also rather limited, restricting the size of projects to those which can be supported by local savings. Where there is already access to markets, marginal farmers may be placed at a disadvantage compared to large farmers. The latter can often buy inputs in bulk and therefore at discount prices. They may have the power to influence decisions on pricing and marketing systems and they can afford to store their produce so as to avoid 'distress' sales at low prices immediately after harvesting.

National agricultural policies, however, can help to encourage farmers to produce a surplus for the cash economy. Since 1981, when the Zimbabwe Government raised the price of maize and abolished controlled pricing mechanisms, peasant farmers there have increased production of maize dramatically. At the same time the Zimbabwe Grain Marketing Board has opened new depots in the communal areas and introduced a new small-scale credit scheme.

An Oxfam Report – *Lands of Plenty, Lands of Scarcity: agricultural policy and peasant farmers in Zimbabwe and Tanzania* – drew attention to the resulting changes: "Peasant farmers, who used to grow mainly for subsistence, are now putting huge quantities of grain on the market ... continuing yearly increases ... show the farmers' confidence in the State marketing and payment system, and also prove that the communal farmer is perfectly capable of increasing production, given the opportunity."

3.2 The inconvenience of formal lending institutions

For many reasons small rural borrowers often prefer borrowing from informal institutions like local moneylenders to taking loans from formal institutions like banks. Although moneylenders levy much higher interest charges, they tend to be more convenient and flexible, and provide more personal service than formal commercial or state institutions.

A survey by Barbara Harriss of small paddy farmers in India found that they had much better access to the private money market than to formal sources of credit. Moneylenders were conveniently located in even the smallest villages. They opened earlier and closed later than banks. They required little or no literacy-demanding paperwork. Often they did not ask for formal collateral. They attended to requests immediately and handed over sanctioned amounts promptly, without retaining a percentage as a deposit. They generally attached no conditions to the use of funds. All of this was in marked contrast to banks' reluctance to extend credit to small farmers and landless labourers.

An Oxfam-commissioned survey carried out by Gramayan in Maharashtra revealed that typical bank loan applications had to be accompanied by eight or more official documents, each requiring costly official stamping. Applicants "had to go 10 to 12 times to the offices at distances of 2 to 55 kms". Processing of loan requests could take between 6 and 16 months and the price for banks' lower interest rates was such that a farmer often had to mortgage his house, bribe various officials and leave 25% of the value of his loan with the bank

as margin money. If his loan was for the purchase of livestock or mechanical equipment he also had to pay for insurance.

Gramayan concluded: "At every stage the farmer has to pay for fees, bribery, travel expenses, cost of refreshment for middlemen and officers, as well as for his own travel and meals. He is obliged to visit banks and other offices frequently and in addition he faces loss of earnings due to absence."

For the small farmers themselves these problems of red tape and general bank reluctance to lend seem insurmountable. For example, delays in responding to credit needs, though sometimes good in that they may force the small farmers to be self-sufficient, often have a very damaging effect. Gramayan's study made this plain: "If a crop loan is delayed the farmer borrows from the moneylender to buy seeds, fertilisers, etc., lest the crop be lost. The interest on this borrowing adds to his costs. If this is not possible his harvest suffers because the inputs (fertilisers, insecticides, etc.) are not applied in time, which again causes loss."

Just as small farmers can be intimidated in their attempts to take bank loans, so, for most commercial banks in poor countries, small farmers and artisans represent undue risk and trouble; positive efforts are needed to persuade them otherwise. This topic is further discussed in Section 4.3.

3.3 The disadvantage of illiteracy

Illiteracy often blocks access to formal institutions for savings and credit and is therefore a problem for many of the people whom Oxfam seeks to help. But ways can be found around the problem.

In 1973 the Self-Employed Women's Co-operative (SEWA) in Ahmedabad started its own co-operative bank. A dispute between SEWA and the Textile Labourers Association (TLA) resulted in the TLA removing its deposit of Rs 700,000 from the bank in 1981. As total deposits then were only about Rs 1,800,000, Oxfam agreed to pay for the salaries of eleven savings-mobilisers who would travel around and about the city, explaining SEWA's methods and objectives and opening and administering small savings accounts.

In order to get around the problem of illiteracy among its clients the society's savings books each included a photograph of the account-holder holding her account number. Bank staff explain verbally procedures for depositing and withdrawing funds to those who cannot read or calculate their balances. In their first year the mobilisers opened 3,000 new savings accounts and raised Rs 1,100,000 in new deposits, more than compensating for the loss of the TLA account.

Although the illiteracy of members of savings and credit schemes can be overcome with a little ingenuity and extra effort, their effective administration will always need at least the skills of reading, writing and basic numeracy. Such schemes are more likely to succeed if all members understand their administration and participate in it. A literacy and/or numeracy programme may be a necessary complement.

An Oxfam study of a co-operative development strategy for Sahelian pastoralists revealed that, while there was active resistance to conventional schooling because it removes children from essential jobs in the herding economy, there was also considerable adult interest in learning to read and write so as to understand, among other things, loan application forms and conditions. It concluded that "functional literacy and numeracy would clearly benefit the administration of projected credit programmes within the herder association structure, for women's groups, herd reconstitution and well construction."

It is also obvious that successful savings and credit schemes need literate, numerate and effective administrators in order to be of enduring benefit. Where illiteracy is widespread, credit schemes should be simplified to avoid legal jargon and unnecessary paperwork, and basic literacy and numeracy relevant to the scheme should be taught.

3.4 Lender prejudices against women

Poverty and illiteracy present serious obstacles to many rural borrowers who hope to obtain formal sector credit. Being a woman adds to those difficulties. Women are frequently denied bank credit altogether, reflecting the chauvinistic assumption that men should control the financial decisions of households. Even if women are in principle permitted to take out loans from banks, other forms of discrimination make it more difficult for them to do so than men. Often, for example, application forms have to be signed by the woman's husband, so that she is unable to take any financial decision without his authorisation.

This bias is often applied against women irrespective of their marital status, so that female-headed households are often refused bank loans. This was the case during the famine in Nyasaland (now Malawi) in 1949. After their husbands had deserted them, or left in search of food, women in the food shortage area found they had lost access to bank credit which was formerly available to them through their husbands. The results illustrate the vital importance of securing access to credit – without their husbands, the women of Nyasaland were unable to borrow the funds they needed to help them through the crisis period, and many of them starved.

3.5 Artificially low interest rates: a deterrent to lenders

Recognising the problems that the rural poor have in obtaining formal credit, many governments have implemented policies which are designed to channel more loan funds in their direction. Often, banks are required to lend to agricultural borrowers at subsidised rates, as in the Indian Differential Interest Rate scheme, which forces state and commercial banks to lend at 4% in rural areas. This reflects the common but misguided assumption that the cost of bank credit is prohibitively high for poorer borrowers.

The problem with this logic is that banks typically perceive poor borrowers as being high-risk borrowers, so that they have strong incentives to avoid lending to the poor at the best of times – and all the more so if the return they receive fails to cover even their basic administration costs. Since it is access to formal credit which is the real problem for the poor, rather than the cost of that credit, enforcing subsidised interest rates is likely to reinforce rather than reverse bank discrimination against poorer borrowers.

Another popular policy attempts to circumvent the problem by restricting loan sizes or imposing loan quotas on banks. But banks may overcome these restrictions by making many small loans to a single wealthy borrower and his family, rather than risk lending to small farmers or the landless who lack adequate collateral. In either case, the rural poor will be driven back into reliance on the local village moneylender, and only the rich will benefit from policies which were intended to help the poor.

Chapter 4

CREDITWORTHINESS

4.1 Collateral security

The standard lender requirement for a deposit or collateral security is a major barrier to institutional credit for marginal farmers, landless labourers and the urban poor. Their lack of assets often forces these groups to rely for working capital on moneylenders, whose security requirements are more flexible, but who often exploit their borrowers' dependence on them. The general advantages which moneylenders gain over formal financial institutions through personal knowledge of borrowers and of localised activities are described by Thomas Timberg and Chandrasekar V Aiyar:

"Informal financial agencies, by and large, concern themselves with the overall credit standing of the borrowing party rather than the specific enterprise or project for which credit is taken ... We asked one broker how he evaluates 'new borrowers' and were told that he never took them; all his clients were children and grandchildren of businessmen with whom he and his father and grandfather had done business."

One way that aid or development agencies can help disadvantaged groups to obtain institutional credit is by giving banks guarantees or deposits on the borrowers' behalf, as Oxfam did for farmers in Andhra Pradesh after the 1977 cyclone. In this case Oxfam placed what were described as 'incentive deposits' with selected banks and persuaded them to lend up to four times this amount to farmers who would otherwise have been denied formal credit. The deposits served as security against default, and the interest paid on them reduced the rate farmers were charged to far below the abnormally high interest rates of the moneylenders. In this way banks can be persuaded to become involved in individual cases; however, they need to change their definition of what constitutes acceptable security if they are to provide this type of credit more generally.

A key form of organisation which avoids the necessity of collateral is the group guarantee; this also has the added advantage of reducing costs of administering small loans to the poor.

One group using group guarantees is the Grameen (Rural) Bank of Bangladesh. This was founded in 1976 by Mohammed Yunus, Professor of Economics at Chittagong University, with the help of an interest-free loan of US $3.4 million from the UN's International Fund for Agricultural Development. The Bank offers credit to the landless and near landless (those with less than 0.4 hectares) for any productive economic activity. Individual borrowers form themselves into groups of five, none of whom can come from the same family, and do business with the bank as a group. The Economist Development Report describes how loans are made:

"The bank gives the group nothing until an official has visited and worked with the members for six weeks to decide whether they are creditworthy. The group has its own bank account into which everyone pays a regular contribution of 1 taka (2 pence). At first only two members of the group can borrow -- and only if their loan application is agreed by the other three members of the group. The next two group members can then apply for a loan only if the first two borrowers have been making their repayments on time for two months. The last member has to wait another two months until his predecessors have passed the reliability test.

"This effectively gets rid of the traditional role of collateral. It makes local pride and peer-group pressure the reasons for paying back a loan, not the threat of losing property ... but this financial caution means that the bank's repayment rates are extraordinary: 98% of loans have been paid back." Compared to a rate of only 50% to 60% for commercial banks in Bangladesh this "suggests that group liability is a better guarantee of financial responsibility than property".

Clearly then, this kind of peer-group pressure can be an effective means of reducing defaults on small loans, and avoids the need for collateral security. It is one of the most successful types of credit delivery to emerge in recent years.

4.2 Income instability of rural borrowers

It is not just because they can offer little security that marginal farmers and the landless appear to be a poor prospect for lenders. Because of the lack of distinction in practice between their 'domestic' and 'production' budgets, unexpected household needs have a direct effect on any formal repayment schedule drawn up in accordance with a 'productive enterprise' budget.

An unforeseen expenditure on a wedding or on medical attention can disrupt repayment of a loan as surely as a delay in harvesting. While these expenditures may be as crucial as the harvest for the long-term future of the household they do not, in the short term, improve productivity. But they nonetheless require suppliers of credit for productive investment to be flexible with regard to disruption of repayment schedules.

In some cases indigenous savings schemes exist (see Section 6.1). These are well suited to funding expenditures which do not occur simultaneously in the community. However, their presence is not a guarantee that production loans will be repaid, due to the order of priority which exists in the 'household economy tree' as discussed in Part 1.

This may mean accepting a delay or irregularities in repayment. In some cases an extra, unplanned credit input may be required.

In 1983 unusually heavy monsoon rains in Western India caused severe flooding in the Marathwada region of Maharashtra. Local voluntary services and Oxfam immediately introduced, amongst other relief and rehabilitation measures, a revolving crop loan scheme.

In spring 1984 the rate of recovery following the first post-flood harvest was nearly 100% in the villages where the scheme was run, but a late monsoon then delayed planting of the second crop of the year until June. As it takes six months for each crop to ripen, without funding the farmers would have lacked the means to plant their next crop. Oxfam granted them a temporary bridging loan of Rs 100,000, almost all of which was repaid.

Income irregularity and seasonal variability may also make it difficult for the rural poor and those in the urban informal sector to make the most of any financial resources by means of small community savings schemes. Some savings and credit co-operatives have tried to overcome the problem.

Although, according to Oxfam's Country Representative in Lusaka, "access to credit is clearly a major constraint on increasing production among subsistence farmers", savings and credit unions (CUs) in north-western Zambia are mostly concentrated among professional workers at the district government offices. This is because the incomes of the rural poor are too low to generate sufficient share capital for CUs to make loans to them. "The seasonality of income among farmers ... makes it difficult for them to contribute regularly to a Credit Union" since most CUs have a minimum monthly contribution.

High costs can be incurred when introducing CUs to the very poor and providing them with adequate training to administer unfamiliar procedures, and a complementary extension and education programme may be required. However, there is one savings and credit union in the area, at Kajibiji settlement, which caters for the needs of small farmers, and it was formed on their own initiative. It recognises that income irregularity makes regular contributions impossible and, with just 15 members, has accumulated 180 kwacha (approximately £100) by allowing members to contribute just two kwacha (£1) "every so often". It aims eventually to use the funds it accumulates to buy a grinding mill for the community.

Both credit and savings schemes can overcome difficulties due to income instability if likely problems are recognised in advance, and if the institutions concerned are prepared to be flexible. In some programmes loans are only given if the income resulting from the loan is sufficient to repay the loan as well as provide an additional income for the borrower. However, this condition can only be applied if a detailed study can be made of the use of the loan and projected income.

4.3 High ratio of transaction costs to loan size

If their input mix is right, marginal farmers can increase productivity quite significantly with the help of very small amounts of credit. From the point of view of banks, however, small loans are less attractive than large ones; since administration costs are relatively fixed regardless of loan size, small loans absorb a proportionately larger slice of the income they generate. Commercial credit institutions need specific inducements to lend to small farmers.

In the 1977 cyclone relief programme in Andhra Pradesh, it was

Oxfam's deposits which persuaded the banks to make loans (Rs 500 per acre, up to a maximum of 2.5 acres) to small farmers replanting their crops, and to relax their normal loan evaluation procedures. Also, the voluntary groups with whom Oxfam was working shared the administrative burden of the loan programme with the banks, although collection of repayments by group workers was criticised to some extent.

UNO is a Brazilian non-governmental organisation in the large city of Recife. It selects promising small businesses, provides considerable consultancy-type help for them and seeks to persuade commercial banks of their viability. By working closely with the banks and providing them with this selection service, it relieves them of both administrative costs and the full burden of risk involved in taking on new accounts.

The industries concerned must go on to achieve independent relationships with the banks, otherwise they are only surviving with effective subsidisation from UNO. Oxfam's Country Representative pointed out this danger:"In a way the banks are on to a good thing – UNO does their work for them and bears the costs of minimising the risks. If UNO were to quit, I can't see the banks taking on the costs of processing small loans."

Some form of mediation between small borrowers and formal sector lenders may be one solution, provided it is clearly limited in its duration and allows borrowers to graduate to full creditworthy status in the bank's eyes, and does not create dependency on the part of the borrowers, on the intermediate agency (see Chapter 9). Another solution may be for borrowers to submit joint applications; costs can be cut by some degree of resource pooling and joint planning, perhaps through a co-operative structure. The use of group guarantees mentioned in Section 4.1 helps to reduce administrative costs.

In deciding how to deal with the high cost of small-scale credit provision, besides using some of the organisational forms suggested, it is crucial to decide whether a minimalist or maximalist approach will be taken. The minimalist approach to credit is to reduce the administrative procedures to the absolute minimum and to reduce the number of questions asked of the prospective borrower. The use to which the loan is put and the question of whether or not it can produce a profit is not of concern in this model. It is argued that analysing individual requests for loans in detail costs more than the slightly increased rate of default which may come about as a result of a less careful consideration of the loan application. The maximalist approach argues that it is unfair on poor people to provide them with credit if there are no opportunities for investment, or if plans for the use of credit are not well prepared. This approach insists upon a detailed scrutiny of each loan application and may include a feasibility study of the proposed use of the credit, with sample income and investment projections alongside profit and loss estimates. Inevitably, the costs of such investigations will be high in relation to small loans.

4.4 Lack of recognition for new community organisations

When individuals cannot obtain credit on their own and decide to approach banks or agencies jointly – as the Grameen Bank encourages them to do – they may still have problems in being recognised as a group. It is not unknown, for instance, for 'co-operatives' to form specifically to gain access to credit, and then disband and vanish on receipt of the funds. As always, the landless have the most difficulty.

For many non-governmental organisations the solution lies in encouraging genuine institution building through informal groups. Even so, until they find means of proving their initiative and viability they will lack credibility with formal institutions and may be required to register as separate legal entities. In Zaire, for example, unless they are registered with the authorities, co-operatives may be considered to be terrorist organisations and can therefore be vulnerable to attack.

The nomadic cattle herders of the Sahel, mentioned in Section 3.3, have no fixed addresses and consequently seem unlikely candidates for credit. Nevertheless, according to an Oxfam report, "herder associations provide a framework which makes credit possible, and experience in Niger indicates that a properly designed credit programme, meeting real needs through herder associations, has high repayment rates, and the necessary financial discipline". If individuals are not in a highly competitive market, they may well be able to provide mutual support to each other.

4.5 Restrictions on loan use

On applying for a formal loan, borrowers typically have to say what they want it for and provide both security and proof that they will be able to repay. Small farmers are usually only granted bank credit for productive, income-generating investment on their farms, not for private consumption.

According to Oxfam's Finance Director:

"Consumption loans are generally thought to be a 'bad thing' by the credit institutions and are therefore generally avoided, but the moneylender, usually successfully, takes a much broader view of the situation. If harvests fail on average once in three years, then three bad years may come in succession and poor farmers will need loans simply to survive. A policy of 'no credit to bad payers' will force them to sell up and move out more quickly than anything, thus making the debts irretrievably lost ... so the provider of rural credit must be prepared to offer the full range of services the moneylender will otherwise provide."

This means having to take a broader view of what is meant by an income-generating purpose. Loans to finance crop storage (perhaps to take advantage of seasonal grain price rises), or to pay off existing high interest debts, may not at first appear to be productive, but they can certainly raise incomes in the longer term. And, in any case, the ultimate effects of even apparently straightforward production loans can be different from their intended purpose, as described in an article by Michael Lipton in World Development (1976):

"The two features of rural lending flows – that they are part of a system of complex personal relations in a village social structure and that they cover consumption as well as investment – have a serious consequence when combined. It is that small sums, injected (e.g. by a rural bank) to provide modern credit for production, may instead strengthen the traditional village system of consumer loans.

"Such outside credit, especially if subsidised, drifts towards the big farmer, who is often a local moneylender; outside credit at 10%, by covering production costs he would have incurred anyway, frees his cash and thus enables him to increase consumption lending at 18-40%. Even if outside credit does go to the small farmer, it may pay him best to repay the moneylender – who then uses it to lend out again to even poorer people, who expect to repay 'interest for ever and capital never'."

Chapter 5

DEFAULT

5.1 The climate, the weather and the seasons

Credit can reduce the risks posed by variations in climatic and seasonal patterns but it cannot remove them. Marginal farmers who join a development scheme, borrow working capital to pay for productivity-boosting inputs (fertiliser, etc.), and then find that abnormal weather delays or destroys the anticipated return on their investments, may be worse off than if they had not joined at all. They will be unable to repay unless they borrow again from another source, almost certainly at a higher interest rate, and in the end will have become more, not less, impoverished.

Thus, certain capital inputs are often needed first if farmers are to reduce their vulnerability to the weather and to improve their creditworthiness for working capital. Irrigation, community wells, pump sets and village grain and seed banks all help to reduce risk and so to increase creditworthiness. Where rural lending is concerned it is partly because of these climatic and seasonal variations that lenders must clearly understand each borrower's capital and working capital investment requirements, even if not called upon to finance both. An imbalance between them may mean that a loan repayment schedule decided on in advance is unfeasible in reality.

Formal lending institutions often have the advantage of extensive branch networks, allowing them to spread risks more widely than localised informal institutions, and so reduce the risk-premium component of their lending rates. This should be an area of agricultural lending in which they are more competitive than moneylenders but there are, as discussed, other factors involved.

5.2 Repayment schedules

Income streams in the rural and urban informal sectors are often irregular, fluctuating widely around the average; yet formal credit institutions often demand a predetermined, constant stream of repayments, without regard to the particular circumstances of individual borrowers. Inflexibility towards unintentional default can turn out to be counter-productive. The moneylender, for example, accepts that crops fail from time to time, and that street vendors experience seasonal income fluctuations, and does not automatically exclude late payers, allowing borrowers to put right in the long run what they cannot avoid in the short term.

However, credit schemes which make outside funds available as part of overall development projects are faced with a dilemma. Those who are excluded for falling behind with repayments, often the poorer participants, are forced back to credit sources which the scheme may have been set up to replace. Yet if permitted to remain as members, the example of delinquency/default may prove infectious.

In the case of Oxfam's rotating crop loans in Andhra Pradesh from 1977 onwards, the first harvest following the cyclone was unfortunately a poor one. The poorest farmers, with few reserves to draw on, could not meet the repayment deadlines and consequently lost their access to cheap credit. Following the delinquency terms of the scheme, one bank did not renew 64% of the interest-free loans in its area for the next planting. Yet by 1982 the overall repayment pattern was far from the picture of mass default which the deadline figures had suggested. With normal interest paid on all outstanding sums from the time they were due, total repayments amounted to around 95% of all borrowers, and 96% of the total sums involved – an excellent record by commercial standards. The rate of repayment on the scheme's follow-up cycles was even better, owing to exclusion of uncreditworthy borrowers at each stage. It is unfortunate that by excluding a high proportion of borrowers from further credit because of late payment (when most of them did pay off their debts in the end), the bank lost potential business and the farmers lost their access to cheap formal sector credit.

5.3 'Soft' lenders

Credit introduced into a community from outside may be perceived quite differently to credit which is, at least partially, locally generated; less responsibility is felt for a stranger's savings than for a friend's or a relative's. Wilful default is also more likely where credit is provided by government or foreign donor agencies than when it is seen to come from commercial banks. (In some South Asian languages, according to Michael Lipton, "the word used for 'loan from the government', tagai or taccavi, means 'assistance, grant', and this confusion of concepts corresponds to major and recurring defaults".)

Borrowers who discover that their credit source is slow to take action against known defaulters, lose motivation in keeping up their own repayments. Thus, lenders should never give the impression of being 'soft' on defaulters. Whenever it is clear that a defaulter has acted deliberately, and not out of sheer desperation, action should be taken to restore good repayment behaviour.

Various deterrents to defaulters can be built into schemes. The desire for a further interest-free bank loan was given as the chief reason for repaying on time by the small farmers in Andhra Pradesh who benefited from Oxfam's post-cyclone revolving crop loan scheme in 1977. Peer-group pressure also improves repayment records. In Andhra Pradesh recipients of the crop loans were obliged to give joint guarantees of security in small groups. If a member did not repay on time he was obliged to pay interest on his loan until it was fully repaid, and in addition all members of his group were denied any further loans from the bank.

Where part of the source of credit is within the community itself, the social pressure to repay is all the greater. The Working Women's Forum, based in the states of southern India, has extended $500,000 worth of credit to groups of between 20 and 30 women. To join, each worker must pay in Rs 6 (30 pence) every month. In return, they are given group passbooks and each member can take out small loans, which must be paid back in ten monthly instalments. The interest rate is only 4-7%, but if an individual defaults, her entire group ceases to be eligible for this advantageous rate.

Specific measures to discourage default can be incorporated in credit schemes, but viable project design and good administration are the most important safeguards. Otherwise, the most successful ways of avoiding default are: group guarantees, serial loans where new loans are only available to those with good repayment records, and good supervision and monitoring.

5.4 Small borrowers' undeserved reputation

Laws which insist that a certain proportion of a bank's loans should be to small agricultural borrowers at concessionary interest rates, naturally tend to bring some less creditworthy borrowers into the formal credit market. Although default rates on loans under this type of scheme are perceived to be higher than for the banks' average loans, the restrictions on interest rates which are imposed deny banks the opportunity to compensate, and may reinforce their prejudices against small rural borrowers.

Yet much evidence suggests that if the design of credit schemes is appropriate for their particular circumstances, and sufficiently flexible, small borrowers are in fact more conscientious about their loan repayments than larger ones. After examining data for India, economist V A Avadhani concluded:

"A larger proportion of farmers repaid loans among marginal, small and medium farmers than among large farmers, both in 1961-62 and 1971-72 ... This would imply that repayment performance of the large cultivators was generally bad in both periods ... richer farmers had defaulted more than smaller cultivators in their repayment performance."

This matches the experience of Oxfam's office in Gujarat, where working capital loans have increasingly been made to very poor village groups and have enjoyed an exceptional overall repayment rate of more than 90%. The Field Staff's close understanding of very poor rural communities has been instrumental in promoting this policy of giving tiny loans for the purchase, for example, of water melon seeds and carpentry tools. This replaces the previous policy, on which default rates were high, of giving relatively large loans for the purchase of milch buffaloes.

Chapter 6

SAVINGS

6.1 Indigenous systems

Indigenous savings systems were discussed to some extent in Chapter 2. It is important to be aware of these before introducing a credit scheme, for two reasons. Firstly, a formal credit scheme may not be necessary if existing mechanisms can be used or adapted. Secondly, a credit scheme may be to the detriment of existing mechanisms and community institutions.

In cash economy societies, savings are deposited with formal institutions such as banks, building societies and post offices. In remote or non-cash societies, indigenous methods such as informal rotating savings clubs often evolve to meet specific local needs. Found in different forms in different countries, they can sometimes be adapted to meet needs other than those for which they were originally devised.

The people of Cameroon employ a cyclical system of savings and credit called the njangi. Every member makes regular contributions, which are collected and distributed to a different member each time, according to a rota devised by the group itself. In effect, those who benefit towards the start of the cycle receive a loan which they repay in instalments, while those towards the end of the cycle are using the system as a means of saving, paying other members before receiving an equivalent sum themselves.

The njangi-type of system is a credit and savings club which requires neither collateral nor formal proof of creditworthiness. Members can join more than one circle at once and can graduate from poor ones to wealthier ones. Literacy is not necessary. Peer-group pressure means default is rare. The njangi mobilises savings to generate credit, and fulfils various social and educational functions too. Similar systems are to be found all over the world. Unless great care is taken, the introduction of a formal credit scheme can damage them. However, it is important not to overestimate the potential of such traditional schemes, which may have very limited and specific uses.

There is a long tradition of savings groups and community activities in Indonesia. A credit and savings group for women in a village in Central Java has enabled these members to set up a group pottery workshop making cooking pots and smokeless stoves.

JEREMY HARTLEY / OXFAM

With appropriate alterations, informal systems of saving can sometimes be adapted to meet new purposes. In Indonesia the arisan informal savings group is similar to the njangi, but is traditionally allocated each time by lot. Changing to a fixed rotation made it suitable for a group of farmers who wished to improve the housing for their cattle. After several cycles, they were able to buy all the necessary materials – cement, timber, and finally roofing. New capital can be added to traditional credit and savings institutions to increase the total credit available to poor people.

Where no such traditional systems exist, or where schemes are not readily adaptable, it may be appropriate to encourage the formation of a broadly based savings and credit society, affiliated to a wider network of Credit Unions. These are popular where the formal financial sector is confined to isolated urban areas and has yet to extend its activities to the remoter and more sparsely populated parts of a country.

6.2 Apparent inadequacy of resources

It is important to distinguish between savings where a surplus is accumulated and savings which represent temporarily postponed expenditure. Mobilising the latent savings potential of a community is an important part of making a development programme independent and self-sustaining. In its request for an Oxfam grant for the salaries of 'savings mobilisers', the Self-Employed Women's Association Bank in Ahmedabad (see Section 3.3) described how, "left to themselves", the poor women it serves "spend any extra money which they make in a particular day". Without any means of accumulating capital sums, the very poor are unable to improve their living conditions.

The very poor are not likely to save when there are more urgent calls on their limited resources. When new schemes for saving are introduced to their communities, it is important that they should be clear and united about the purpose, and committed to it. Furthermore, because the sums that the very poor are able to save regularly are tiny, formal savings institutions find that the value of such small accounts is outweighed by the cost of administering them, and consequently neglect them. For several reasons, it may prove difficult to realise the savings potential of very poor people who lack appropriate indigenous methods.

Self-administered schemes, however, can bridge the gap between the informal and formal savings sectors and, with the help of one or other of them, members of informal savings clubs can together accumulate sufficient sums to gain entry to formal institutions.

Saveway clubs in Southern Africa have their origins in the credit and savings societies devised by the Institute of Adult Education at the University of Zimbabwe, and promoted in the former'Tribal Trust Lands' in the early 1970s. Guidelines and stationery for them, in a revised form, were made more generally available through Oxfam's Field Offices. Community groups are encouraged to decide upon a purpose for saving, and then to go about it using a system of stamps, certificates and passbooks, which Oxfam at first provided free.

The system is designed to be administered by members of the group themselves at weekly meetings, and to help them save for collective objectives of benefit to them all. The sums collected at each meeting can be banked together in one account with a formal savings institution, although the club maintains its own separate records for each member. The value of the clubs is twofold: they introduce the savings habit to groups whose primary purpose is not savings (church groups, workers' associations, etc.) and they also act as a catalyst for

independent, small-scale institution building. However, such schemes are less successful in areas where high inflation can reduce the value of cash savings

6.3 The discouraging effect of cheap credit

Grants or injections of credit may reduce a community's commitment to building and maintaining its own savings mechanisms. Thus, there is a danger that introducing credit or subsidies without taking savings into account may induce undesirable dependency; it may also affect attitudes to risk-taking. This was commented on by Oxfam's Finance Director, after a tour of projects in India:

> *"Many of the loan schemes tempted marginal farmers with small amounts of land to take risks they would not normally contemplate and I suspect they felt little involvement with the inevitable failures. Where a farmer had given some security, however, he was absolutely worse off than before if he failed; the loss of his security (usually land) would also affect his future earning power or would force him to make repayments from future income. Risks taken with savings, on the other hand, are likely to be entered into with a much stronger sense of commitment and any loss thereof (though regrettable) will not constrict his future income in the same way."*

Where any capacity for savings exists – and there are very few situations in which there is none at all – people should be encouraged to generate as much as possible of the sum they need from their own resources. Otherwise, the problem remains that while the use of credit may lift them to a higher standard of living, it may also land them more heavily in debt.

In some areas there have recently been attempts to introduce selective subsidised credit as an incentive to agricultural production. To ensure the desired impact of the subsidy, it is often only made available once the loan has been repaid and agricultural produce harvested, so that it acts as a bonus to someone successfully utilising the loan. This type of subsidy can have the disadvantage described for 'conditional loans' and may be more useful for the slightly more affluent peasant farmer.

In many programmes it has been realised that savings can become an integral part of a credit programme and together they can encourage the accumulation of capital in a community.

Chapter 7

PROGRAMME DESIGN

7.1 Lenders' assumptions

Large farmers are generally assumed to have adequate access to commercial credit; small farmers and landless labourers, on the other hand, are considered high-risk borrowers and therefore are denied formal sector credit. In recent years governments and other organisations in poor countries have been concerned to correct this institutional bias, and to improve the availability of formal sector credit to small farmers. Lending policies, however, continue to reflect commonly-held assumptions about them, which are often simplistic or even completely incorrect.

Small farmers are often assumed to have little capacity for voluntary savings. Their lack of assets forces them to borrow from moneylenders, who exploit them with unduly high interest rates. So outside agencies tempt them to invest in potentially profitable new techniques and machinery with offers of attractively cheap subsidised credit. The intention is to release them from the clutches of moneylenders by means of profitable innovations.

However, this focus on the supply of rural credit can distract attention from farmers' needs as they themselves perceive them. While credit can alleviate some of their problems, it is not a complete solution and will rarely succeed without appropriate complementary inputs. Its virtual imposition may also be counter-productive. If a moneylender is also a trader or employer, credit policies which drive him out of business may be beneficial in one respect, but damaging in another. In designing credit-based programmes, lenders need to understand the circumstances prevailing in each situation if credit is to be used successfully for the purpose for which it is intended.

7.2 Specific purpose credit (conditionality)

Lenders often designate the purpose for which loans are to be used as a means of reducing the risk of default. In practice, however, it is almost impossible for outsiders to control the use to which additional household liquidity is put, even with loans in kind.

Unless borrowers and lenders happen to have a precisely similar view of household expenditure priorities, they need to work together to obtain a comprehensive mutual understanding before they tie credit to a particular productive purpose. This involved approach requires a consortium of reliable institutions including the government and banks. Without mutual agreement about its use, specific purpose credit is more likely to meet an institution's lending criteria than a borrower's real needs, producing unforeseen results. If borrowers find they are forced to make unfamiliar investments, the outcome may distort the household or community economy to their disadvantage.

Since credit should only be given for activities which raise net incomes and generate repayment capacity, the principle on which it is granted should be flexible conditionality. Borrowers should be allowed to identify productive investment opportunities open to them, rather than having development 'packages' thrust upon them.

In 1964 the Syndicate Bank in Karnataka decided that there was untapped potential for agricultural lending in India, and set up the Syndicate Agriculture Foundation to support its programme of farm lending. The Foundation opened 'farm clinics' next to Bank branches to select and recommend prospective small borrowers, whom they then continued to provide with extension services and technical help. An Oxfam grant enabled the Foundation to purchase visual aid materials for its programme of education and training.

A farm clinic also holds stocks of material inputs which are used as bank credits, and its agricultural advisers instruct borrowers on the techniques of using them. The Bank's confidence in its ability to raise borrowers' productivity is clear from its provision of housing loans to persuade them to stay and cultivate their plots, which might be neglected if they left in search of wage employment.

Without this kind of active involvement, conditionality can cause credit schemes to go badly astray. If borrowers have requirements (perhaps to pay for a wedding or a funeral) which they believe are more urgent than inputs (e.g. fertiliser) provided by lenders, they may divert some of the latter in order to pay for the former. If high-yielding seeds are planted without fertiliser, for example, they can result in a worse harvest than if indigenous seed had been used, leaving the farmer who borrowed to pay for them unable to repay.

Loans in kind are often used to try to enforce conditionality, but they are an undesirable way of extending credit to poor people unless there are positive reasons for using them. They may be appropriate in the aftermath of a disaster or in a situation in which distribution problems have caused normal sources of inputs to run short; they may also be used where a monopoly supplier chooses to restrict supply or raise prices unduly. Where loans in kind are used, borrowers should be encouraged after the first instance to procure supplies of the input for themselves, perhaps forming buyer groups so as to obtain bulk-buying discount prices.

7.3 Credit alone is not enough

A development plan which is designed without much consultation with its proposed beneficiaries, or which introduces previously unknown techniques, may fail by neglecting vital aspects of the problem. For beneficiaries who rely on credit in order to participate in such a plan its failure is particularly disastrous. At best they will be sceptical of further development schemes, at worst chronically indebted; and if the loans are written off, the development agency acquires a reputation for being 'soft'. It is of particular importance to ensure that 'crop' or production credit is related to other inputs, even more so than with fixed capital credit (tools).

Agricultural credit schemes need to have all the necessary inputs from the start if they are to succeed. An Oxfam adviser in Zaire, Dr B N Okwuosa, wrote a paper on livestock production in 1975 in which he said: "To have a successful credit programme, it will have to be an integral part of a rural development programme: i.e. there must be supporting services, a viable market, price incentives, good infrastructure and extension services ... Many credit programmes in developing countries have failed because some of these points have been neglected." Oxfam has since followed this approach in its rural programme in Zaire.

Oxfam's five-year programme of support for two ox traction centres in the fertile and under-populated Kasai Occidental region near the Angolan border has helped to raise the incomes of small cultivators by increasing by 350% the area of land each household can cultivate.

Before being given credit to purchase ox traction equipment, co-operative groups, made up of seven or more households, must first cultivate their lands communally for two growing seasons and prove they can market the proceeds by putting up 25% of the cost of the

equipment themselves. **They repay in four instalments over two years, one after each harvest. But credit is only one part of the programme. The ox traction centres' main role is in training before providing the oxen and equipment and in a continuing advisory service afterwards. They teach veterinary and agricultural skills and also give instruction in carpentry, equipment maintenance and book-keeping.**

In small-scale programmes the provision of credit alone is rarely sufficient for genuine development. For example, a loan made by Oxfam to landless labourers in Gujarat, so that they could sink a well and start farming some waste land the Government had granted them, was not repaid; the recipients were given minimal extension help, even though they had little knowledge of the land or how to improve it. Since credit is so often linked to innovation, training is perhaps its most important complement.

In 1977, two planting projects in Orissa, one after a drought and the other after flooding, did not meet with much success. Oxfam's assistant representative there later wrote about their potentially innovative nature. "In the first case, a disaster was used to introduce a new crop (HYV Winter Wheat), new techniques and new inputs. Similarly, the second project introduced a new variety (Culture-28), plus a new concept, that of a revolving loan fund. All this was done with the greatest of speed and with no input or time for farmer education.

"Lack of an agricultural extension component meant that ... farmers were partly responsible for their own low yields. To this day the villagers spoken to do not understand how a revolving loan fund should operate. One wonders what affect the initial, organised introduction of a social (or educational) component ... would have made to the development of these programmes."

Rural credit schemes risk falling short of their objectives unless the training and the physical inputs necessary are clearly perceived at the outset, and comprehensive provision is made for them.

Similarly, credit alone is unlikely to be successful if the prices paid to the poor are inadequate, transport and market demand insufficient and raw materials unavailable.

A trainee at the ox-traction centre in Kasai, Zaire. Besides learning how to look after and use a team of oxen, trainees are taught carpentry skills so that they can make and repair ploughs and ox-carts.

41

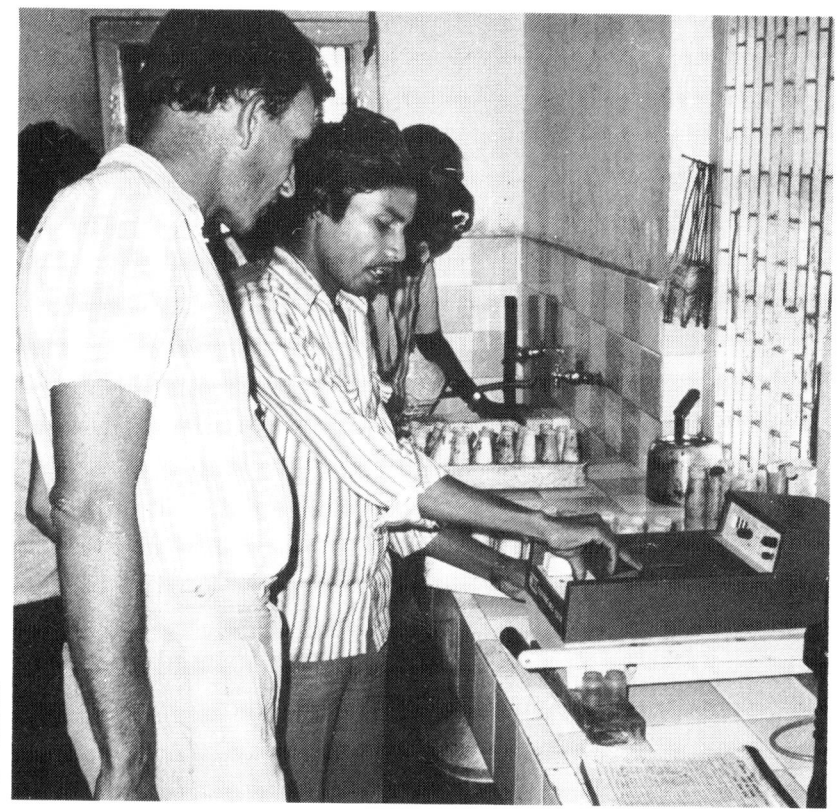

Testing the fat content of milk at the dairying project in Gujarat. Proven quality means farmers are paid more for their milk.

7.4 Appraisal and monitoring

Careful appraisal and monitoring makes the difference between success and failure for both grants and credit. The following example illustrates the disastrous consequences of a complete lack of project appraisal.

> **When they first decided to form a poultry co-operative, the poor women of Phansa, in Gujarat, did not realise that their bank would retain 15% of the loan they took to start it as security. Finding themselves short of working capital they managed to obtain a loan of Rs 25,000 from Oxfam.**

42

It was Gujarat's only womens' poultry co-operative, and inexperience obliged the women to hand the young chicks over to a commercial poultry for rearing. More serious than the additional expense this incurred was the state of the chickens when they returned; their growth was stunted by poor feeding, their laying life much diminished. To make matters worse, egg prices fell by 44% and at the same time feed prices went up by 50%.

The chickens, through no fault of their own, proved unable to achieve the laying rates required to meet the bank's repayment schedule. Only replacement of the whole flock could have reversed the decline in egg production; the co-operative collapsed, its members recriminating among themselves and hopelessly in debt.

Sometimes projects can be 'rescued' by monitoring:

The introduction of dairying is one way of raising the incomes of poor and landless people, and dairying enjoys some popularity in southern Gujarat. However, repayment rates on the buffalo loan schemes which Oxfam funded were disappointing; in 1981 the Behavioural Sciences Centre in Ahmedabad was commissioned to study the causes. Its report blamed the generally poor productivity in milk production on low yields, unduly short lactation periods and high buffalo mortality, all resulting from inadequate nutrition. Noting that dairying was quite a new concept for the people of the area, it recommended better training in animal husbandry and veterinary care, and increased provision of green fodder and supplementary feeding for the buffaloes.

In poor countries, project holders' lack of financial skill and technical expertise may mean that adequate appraisal and monitoring of rural credit programmes are difficult, but the vulnerability of participants in the case of failure make these procedures of crucial importance. Participatory research may provide an answer to this need and suggested guidelines for this are given in the Appendix.

7.5 Capital rationing and project ranking

All development agencies have limited funds to dispense among a large number of deserving projects. They have to evaluate each application for funding on its merits and also to decide at which point to discontinue funding in order to divert their scarce resources elsewhere. Continual evaluation and appraisal is required. Unlike a commercial organisation, Oxfam does not rank the priority it attaches to projects in declining order of return on investment, but according to the urgency of beneficiaries' needs.

There may be conflict in the minds of those who decide on the allocation of resources between benefiting those whose need is evidently greatest and those whose ability to repay is anticipated to be best. Experience shows that poor borrowers can often put small loans to very effective use (e.g. for craft materials or 'liberation loans' – see Section 9.2), that they tend to have better repayment records than larger borrowers (Section 5.4) and that, if loans are properly monitored, they are the most worthy recipients of credit on both counts

Chapter 8

PARTICIPATION

8.1 No commitment without participation

Governments and development agencies often approach rural
communities with a conviction that they know what is best for the
community's 'development' and 'modernisation'. The paternalistic or
even mildly authoritarian strategies which result may mean that the
people at the base of the community concerned have few opportunities
for participating in defining goals, determining procedures, or controlling
or evaluating the activities of the organisations which represent them.

Yet only if all the beneficiaries design and implement a programme
themselves is it likely to meet their real needs and to enable them all to
share in its benefits. Motivation and commitment result from such
participation.

Analysis of the two crop credit schemes in Orissa (referred to in Section
7.3) attributes their failure to lack of participation. "The beneficiaries were
not actively involved in planning, implementation or control ... outsiders
devised the programme and administered it. In part, this may be a
problem with many programmes in the wake of a disaster, but the
organisational structure should allow for changes and adjustments as the
situation improves, and on the basis of feedback information."

The evaluator of Oxfam's revolving crop loan schemes after the 1983
floods in Marathwada (referred to in Section 4.2), found that they were
designed and run almost entirely by the chosen voluntary groups, with
hardly any input from the beneficiaries; the latter, by implication as a
consequence, were unwilling to become involved in running them. It is
clear that schemes without a measure of participation may simply
substitute new forms of dependency for old ones, without bringing any
substantial shift towards self-sufficiency and independence.

One of the most common ways of obtaining rural credit is through
credit co-operatives. If well administered and properly organised they can
be important vehicles for engaging the participation of the borrowers.

8.2 Distinguishing different needs within borrower groups

Involving the people concerned as closely as possible in the design as well as the implementation of credit-based development, helps to ensure that it is they, and not others, who actually benefit from it. Whatever the plan of a programme, it rarely turns out to the disadvantage of those with responsibility for implementing it. If it relies on existing local traditional leaders, it will probably serve their best interests, among which greater economic independence and a better standard of living for the poorest may not necessarily feature prominently, and the programme effects may turn out to be the opposite of what the original planners envisaged. The local economic power structure should therefore be analysed to ensure that the poor do not actually suffer from the proposed intervention.

Needs for credit may be perceived differently by different members of the same household. The inability of many African countries to feed their people is partly explained by neglect of the role of women in food production. Women, according to UN statistics, produce 60-80% of food for the family. Yet often they have access neither to credit nor markets, and may not even be allowed to choose which crops to plant. If their husbands, encouraged by the provision of cheap credit to grow a particular crop for the market, insist that it is planted on the whole of their plot, women are unable to plant what their families need to eat.

A clear understanding is needed of each community involved in a credit scheme, especially its social structures and its power relationships. Depending on the groupings of borrowers within it, effective administration may require a measure of small-scale institution building. The Grameen Bank of Bangladesh (Section 4.1) makes its tiny loans to very poor, mainly landless, people in groups of five at a time. They are required to organise themselves into these groups, to agree on a plan with which to approach the Bank.

The development economist John Madeley describes how, as a result:

"... loans have been given for over 300 different and varied activities: trading purposes, making processed goods, providing transport services, storing agricultural produce, marketing farm inputs and outputs, and for maintenance services. Comparatively few loans are taken out directly for agricultural purposes – but agriculture is receiving much of the benefit from the higher incomes the scheme is helping to generate."

By way of contrast, both Oxfam's planting schemes in Orissa (Sections 7.3 and 8.1) were directed at larger and less homogeneous groups;

Oxfam's Assistant Country Representative later ascribed many of their difficulties to this fact:

"Since the programmes' structure was community based rather than based on a particular social or economic class (where there are more likely to be feelings of common identity and solidarity), this mixed membership neutralised any social pressure that a group as a whole could otherwise place on defaulters. More importantly, perhaps, it also meant that genuine village organisations controlled by the people could never be formed.

"Where the wealthy have influence and power over the poor and often feel little responsibility towards them, then including them within an organisation inevitably results in their taking control. Large farmers have greater effective access to institutional credit and can anyway often withstand the loss of one crop without hardship."

He admits that both project holders were initially vague as to who the beneficiaries were, but that over 10% in one project and "a significant number" in the other were large landowners; "their inclusion was unnecessary in both programmes, and increased [the programmes'] complexity and size".

While he recognises the detailed local knowledge required, Oxfam's Country Representative in Gujarat considers that credit-based programmes should only be directed to the poorest people, who must organise themselves with leaders from among their number. Very small loans to small groups are highly productive; the return is greater in terms of improvement to their standard of living than for wealthier borrowers, and repayment rates (in Gujarat at least) are very high.

However, as the poorest households lack the resources to pay for many of their needs, the less directly responsible they are for the administration of schemes offering them credit for productive purposes, the greater the likelihood that they will somehow or other divert such credit to other purposes. If credit schemes are to succeed in helping very poor beneficiaries, they need to be capable of generating particularly strong commitment to the achievement of their objectives.

In summary, it would be best not to mix rich and poor in credit schemes, especially where the rich can monopolise the new resources. The most positive programmes have been those in which more homogeneous groups have worked together. This may also entail encouraging groups for women only, to ensure they have full access to the programme.

8.3 Training in administration and financial techniques

Efficient administration is vital for all savings and credit schemes. This means at the very least keeping an accurate record of payments and receipts. The more beneficiaries understand administration and participate in it, the less the likelihood of errors of accountability. Traditional informal savings and credit systems, like njangi and arisan, rely on simplicity and openness to put accountability beyond question and to retain their members' confidence. In general, the simpler and more open the system, the better its chances of success.

Many credit-based schemes fail because of their beneficiaries' and project holders' poor understanding of procedure. This was Oxfam's experience in the 1980 planting project in Orissa (Section 7.3) where, according to the Assistant Representative, "the President had not kept accurate records and gave out loans to all who approached him ... a number of different family members would come forward separately for a loan. The project had not collected any production figures from the crop but still stated that production was between 12 and 24 quintals per acre when the maximum average yield ... is 12 quintals per acre with optimum inputs and favourable weather." (1 quintal = 100 kg.)

It may be that some projects would benefit from more regular checks by officials of funding agencies, but the smaller the project, the less time they can generally afford to spend on it. Accountability can only really be improved in the long term if both beneficiaries and administrators are schooled in appropriate financial techniques. Performance can be improved through simple courses in book-keeping, and where it is not possible to set up savings and credit schemes directly, they can be encouraged indirectly through specialist training centres, whose pupils can go on to introduce efficiently-administered schemes in their own home areas.

The savings and credit co-operatives organised by village and employee groups in some West African countries offer members the chance to accumulate personal savings and enjoy a source of credit, whilst still retaining democratic control of the administration and allocation of resources. The main problem in credit unions is to find active members who are sufficiently educated in operational techniques of financial management. Most school teachers, extension workers, agency officials and volunteers do not have the specialist knowledge, time and resources to help.

The African Co-operative Savings and Credit Association (ACOSCA) has responded by establishing training centres, among them one at Bamenda in Cameroon, where co-op officials are taught, among other things, about book-keeping, auditing, handling delinquency, community development and leadership. National credit union organisations put students forward for courses; after training they return to run their local credit union or co-op. Many credit unions have been established in West and Central Africa as a result of the activities of these training centres.

The benefits of investment in training are long-term and produce a less immediate and readily quantifiable return than direct investment in production credit schemes. But no credit-based scheme can become truly self-administering and independent without a firm basis of training in the particular managerial and technical skills applicable, as well as in credit control and accounting.

After a report on deficiencies in schemes for buffalo dairying which involved credit (Section 7.3), Oxfam funded field teams from the Behavioural Sciences Centre in Ahmedabad to conduct village training camps and demonstration projects for milk co-operatives. Training in credit administration is only of use if its participants are also properly trained in the purposes for which credit is given.

Training as a supplement to credit will be particularly important for poor women, who may suffer from lower general levels of education and literacy than men. This lack of literacy skills may also reduce their confidence and willingness to expand their economic activity to a level where it is of sufficient size to produce enough income to keep them and their dependents.

8.4 Replication of existing power relationships

A problem with all new informal institutions designed to remedy the deficiencies of the formal financial sector is that they often mirror the power and status relationships which already exist within their communities, and this can reduce their ability to make social and economic progress for their members.

Oxfam's West Orissa Programme (OXWORP), which included various credit-based schemes, was designed to help develop an entire region of Orissa State. It was implemented through management committees, to be set up in each selected village and to be run by the villagers themselves. The committees were intended to identify local needs and to represent each section of a village's population in funding negotiations with OXWORP's central administration.

A major evaluation report later revealed that many management committees simply reflected local power or caste relations, and that they tended to be dominated by those whose motives were self-advancement, not community development.

"Many committees have faced the dilemma of deciding whether a particular course of action should be judged in terms of the welfare of the committee or the welfare of the village. This might not have been a problem if all those who could be regarded as poor were, in fact, members of the committees; as it is, however, few committees have been able to draw all the poor together.

"The question naturally arises then as to whether the assistance given to the committee really reached those for whom the programme was originally intended." The report then refers to the situation on one particular village committee: "It did not go unnoticed that the principal office bearers were able to adopt a more affluent lifestyle and this tended somewhat to destroy the confidence that the membership had in them."

So, added to the committee members' inability to agree on projects of benefit to all villagers was an unhealthy degree of corruption and nepotism; furthermore their positions were often entrenched by a virtual monopoly of literacy and numeracy skills.

Thus it appears that it can be just as difficult to make credit available to the poorest through informal institutions as it is through banks. Credit schemes, co-operatives and the like, when they involve the poorest working together to reduce their economic dependence, are seen as a threat by those in a position of power. Consequently the latter do all they can to prevent such schemes from being successful, sometimes by manipulating them to their advantage as seen in the OXWORP example. In these cases political change is often necessary before the poor can assume control over their own lives.

Chapter 9

DEPENDENCY

9.1 Impediments to self-sufficiency

Outside assistance may discourage communities which are largely capable of helping themselves from doing so, and generate undesirable dependence on further inputs. A revolving credit scheme which is based on concessionary rates of interest, for example, only lasts while subsidised funds are available; inflation means periodic additional inputs are required if it is to continue, let alone expand.

Most development projects have indirect as well as direct elements (administration, training, etc.) which are sometimes hidden, but without which the direct part of the scheme would cease to be viable. Ideally, if schemes are eventually to become self-supporting, participants need to be aware of both elements, and to assume responsibility for them both.

Credit for any borrower whom a bank would consider too risky or not worthwhile, even at a high commercial rate, is effectively subsidised credit. An 'incentive deposit', or guarantee to a bank to facilitate credit for borrowers who lack the necessary collateral security themselves, is a form of hidden subsidy.

A subsidy, hidden or otherwise, can create dependency which may inhibit, rather than promote, the objective of self-sufficiency for its recipients in the long term. An Oxfam Country Representative summed up the dilemma: "The important question for Oxfam is whether we are really doing a group a favour by giving it a 'subsidised' loan if our aim is to get them used to the competitive commercial world, or are we merely postponing the day when they have to face economic reality." Evaluation of Oxfam's Andhra Pradesh 'incentive deposit' scheme reached generally positive conclusions, noting that as a result some small farmers established permanent relationships with banks, but it added that some "became dependent, as they kept looking for somebody to help them in approaching the banks". Similarly, the scheme had created a "dependency of banks on an intermediary agency for security"; they were reluctant to offer loans to the same extent without further 'incentive deposits', driving farmers back to their former dependence on moneylenders.

It can be concluded from points made both here and earlier in the text that direct subsidies should be avoided as they inevitably create dependency. However, the effects of indirect/hidden subsidies are less clear cut; the training of 11 women as mobilisers in SEWA – in effect, a hidden subsidy – has not resulted in dependency, but has had very positive consequences. 'Liberation loans', also hidden subsidies, often effectively reduce dependency, as seen in Section 9.2. In the last analysis, the continuity of credit is more important to the poor than a short-term subsidy.

9.2 The need to generate income growth

Without adequate design or supervision there is always the danger that a credit scheme can be diverted from its intended purpose and fail to generate sufficient return to make repayments (Section 7.2). An enterprise which has enough fixed capital cannot generate an adequate return if it is short of working capital, and vice versa; a request for one type of capital, therefore, should be examined in the light of whether there is an adequate supply of the other. It is naturally easier to appraise working capital requirements than projects for fixed capital investment.

In 1977, basket workers from Himatnagar Taluka in Gujarat formed a co-operative in order to obtain a government bamboo quota. Its business expanded and the co-operative approached the Government for a working capital loan, but then ran into difficulties, explained by an Oxfam Country Representative: "The Handicrafts Board, a Government agency, allocated about Rs 9,000 as working capital and released Rs 2,500 of it to the co-op. The co-op purchased bamboo with it. They subsequently purchased a truck load of bamboo from Rajpipla worth about Rs 6,500 at a cheaper rate. They were depending on the balance from the Handicrafts Board to pay for it but the agency refused to release any further money until the original amount of Rs 2,500 has been returned. This made nonsense of allocating Rs 9,000 as working capital!"

The co-op approached Oxfam for a loan to make up the difference between what they had received and what they had actually been promised and needed. It was granted, and a year later the Country Representative reported again: "With the Oxfam loan of Rs 5,000 given last year, the co-operative purchased 3,700 bamboos which were distributed to 55 members. **From these bamboos the members produced goods worth Rs 16,100 and made a total profit of Rs 1,581 (Rs 5,000 was returned last December as requested by us).**"

It is widely held that credit schemes for the very poor should only promote investment in productive purposes, since unless people increase their very low incomes they will be unable to repay. However, credit can sometimes generate income growth without being used for orthodox productive investments. 'Liberation loans' substitute realistically priced working capital for capital which has previously only been available from one source at a high rate of interest, and thus free borrowers from a state of enforced dependency. For example, marginal farmers without access to formal credit channels might be able to use such a loan to increase their income by paying off their high interest debts.

The plight of Kottar's fishermen is described in an Oxfam Project brief. "The fishermen are poor, their earnings are uncertain, they have no security and only a few have their own nets and boats. They have to borrow from local merchant moneylenders in order to buy a net or a catamaran, with the condition that they must sell their catch to the merchant who financed them and who pays considerably below the market price of the fish. Loans can carry up to 100% interest, and when the fishermen need money to buy new equipment, for a marriage or even for food in the lean season, they are obliged to borrow further. Thus the fishermen are caught in a net of poverty and are exploited by the merchants to whom they are constantly in debt." The Kottar Social Service Society encouraged the formation of co-operatives – sangams – to act as marketing outlets and savings banks in order to end the fishermen's dependence on the merchant moneylenders, but the sangams stipulated that members had to be free from debt. After Oxfam had placed a deposit with it as security, a bank agreed to provide credit at moderate interest rates so that the fishermen could pay off the moneylenders and be free to sell their catches at open market prices. In turn, they were able to pay off the bank loans within two years, and become full members of the sangams.

Credit used to free workers from situations of enforced dependency like this, or even from bonded labour, has a doubly liberating effect if it releases enough suppressed income-earning capacity to enable workers to pay back loans long before their term of 'bondage' would have expired.

It is important to realise that for the poor the distinction between what are productive assets and what is consumption may be unclear. For example, a loan for a house roof can be regarded as unproductive but if the house is also used for weaving or some other economic activity, then the roof will enhance the work place and keep the stock dry. Similarly, a cooker may be used to feed the family but also to bake bread for sale on the streets. A loan for such an investment may have to be scrutinised in terms of its dual purpose. It is perhaps easier to visualise the role of credit for the very poor in terms of removing constraints on income generation, rather than as straight investment in specific productive enterprises.

9.3 Institutionalising dependence

Individuals and communities lack real independence until they develop the means of saving (with a reasonable margin for error) at times when they enjoy an excess of income over expenditure for times when expenditure necessarily exceeds income. Unless the communities exist in isolation, this means establishing a measure of equilibrium over a sustained period between requirements from the wider world and contributions to it.

Credit-based programmes must develop local mechanisms for saving and must train the beneficiaries to run the programmes themselves. Otherwise, they simply institutionalise dependence on assistance from outside the community; no group will be properly independent until they can outgrow this reliance.

> **The reliance of small Haitian coffee growers in the remote area of Carice on seasonal loans (at 100% interest) from coffee speculators was noted by a local church mission. Oxfam made a grant to the mission to establish a revolving crop loan fund to break this dependency and went on to fund other projects in what was described as an integrated rural development programme.**
>
> **After several years of support, funding stopped when it became apparent that the mission had not succeeded in building effective local savings and credit mechanisms and that its educational programme continued to be reliant on agronomists and animators from outside the community. The mission did not set limits to either**

Weighing a coffee crop at the Co-operative office in Carice, Haiti. The co-operative offers fair prices for the crop and gives cash advances to members if necessary.

the duration or the extent of outside involvement; it was felt that the role of the mission was effectively being institutionalised.

Undue reliance on the leadership of a particular individual creates conditions similar to dependency on outside institutions. Ideally, no one personality should be indispensable to a community, because when their organising abilities are no longer available, their work will be at risk unless a successor can be found. It is better, but more complicated, to promote broadly-based community development. A team of potential successors should be trained at the earliest opportunity.

The success of the Mulkanoor co-operative, which remains the main source of inspiration for India's multi-co-op movement despite the failure of many other similar ventures, is said to be largely due to the effectiveness of its president. The growth of the Grameen Bank in Bangladesh owes a great deal to the energy of its founder, Professor Mohammed Yunus. With development projects such as these, in both of which credit plays a major role, it is important that the inspiration and drive of charismatic leaders are supported from an early stage by the efforts of like-minded supporters, who are both committed to continuing the work, and capable of doing so. Otherwise, despite all the people who have come to rely on them, anything they achieve may not endure.

Conclusion

Attempts to offer very poor people the chance of a better livelihood by the introduction of new ways of saving and obtaining credit have often run into difficulties. That does not mean that the principle is wrong; many credit and savings schemes have succeeded in raising living standards and in promoting community development. For people with almost no resources of their own who are seeking to raise their level of income, some form of credit is vital. The conclusion drawn here is that the role of small-scale credit and savings schemes in the development process is crucial; and that their effectiveness can be enhanced and their impact maximised if the following points are borne in mind with regard to design and administration.

1. Credit is usually extended as one element of a plan to introduce new and improved production methods, so the scheme as a whole must be viable. If it lacks important inputs, or if insufficient credit is allowed, the credit element will fail along with the rest of the scheme.

2. Credit does not necessarily imply the provision of loan funds. Given encouragement, many communities can provide their members with funds for investment through communal saving systems, and agencies can often tap formal institutions for funds for small borrowers by acting as guarantors or intermediaries.

3. Credit is in any case only viable in conjunction with schemes which include an adequate programme of training. Participants need to understand fully any new techniques involved and, where appropriate, to have access to extension services.

4. Credit itself may be a foreign concept; beneficiaries should understand their obligations clearly and be trained in book-keeping. Accounts fulfil the double function of both informing lenders and also encouraging financial discipline among borrowers, so they should be compiled and published regularly.

5. Credit-based development schemes are more likely to achieve their objectives where their beneficiaries are not just consulted about their

needs, but also participate actively in design and in administration. The process helps project-managers to avoid making errors and assumptions about the social and economic background.

6. Default is often a sign that insufficient attention has been paid to either design, or monitoring, or both. If default is not to spread, rapid remedial action is needed.

7. Interest should be charged to mitigate the effects of inflation and to encourage a sense of independence. The equivalent of the local bank rate for personal loans would be appropriate. A project which cannot support a reasonable rate of interest (in kind if necessary) is not viable for credit finance.

8. Small-scale schemes for the very poor, if properly administered, can be the most rewarding ones in terms of the improvement to their living conditions, the building of new community structures, and repayment records.

It would perhaps be helpful to get away from the notion of a 'credit programme', and instead to see credit as simply one tool, albeit a powerful one, in integrated programmes of development.

Sources and References

Published and unpublished books and articles:

Avadhani V A, 'Rural retrogression and institutional finance', *Economic and Political Weekly*, June 1979.

Bouman and Harteveld, 'The njangi: a traditional form of saving and credit in West Cameroons', *Sociologica Ruralis* Vol.XVI, 1976.

Copestake J, 'Loans for Livelihoods: government sponsored credit schemes, India', unpublished manuscript, University of Reading 1987.

Fuglesang A, Chandler D, *Participation as Process: what we can learn from Grameen Bank, Bangladesh*, NORAD, Oslo 1987.

Gramayan, *Problems Faced by Small Farmers and Agricultural Labourers in Obtaining Bank Loans,* (distributed by Oxfam office, Nagpur).

Harper M, *Small Business in the Third World: guidelines for practical assistance,* John Wiley and Sons, New York 1984.

Harriss B, 'Money and commodities, monopoly and competition',in *Borrowers and Lenders,* ed. Howell, ODI 1985.

Jackson T and Park P, *Lands of Plenty, Lands of Scarcity: agricultural policy and peasant farmers in Zimbabwe and Tanzania,* Oxfam 1985.

Lipton M, 'Agricultural finance and rural credit in poor countries', *World Development* Vol.4, no.7, 1976.

Madeley J, 'Credit where it's needed, in three Asian countries', *International Agricultural Development* Vol.4, no.4, July 1984.

Pratt B S and Boyden J, eds, *Oxfam Field Directors' Handbook,* Oxfam 1985.

Timberg and Aiyar, 'Informal credit markets in India', *Economic and Political Weekly,* May 1980.

Young L, 'A report on the use of agricultural credit for poor disaster victims in India', *Disasters,* March 1983.

cont....

Confidential unpublished Oxfam evaluations:

Project study (1983)

Evaluation of savings and credit in rural Bangladesh (1985)

Confidential Oxfam project files:

Brazil 130; Burkina Faso 123; Cameroons 17,22; Gujarat 43, 46, 80, 86, 98, 99, 112, 114, 133, 155;   Haiti 52, 53; Indonesia 166; Karnataka 46, 59; Maharashtra 80, 110; Tamil Nadu 2; Zaire 165; Zambia 56.

NOTE: *Because of the confidential nature of the evaluations and project files, access is restricted to personal callers at Oxfam House in Oxford, by previous arrangement with Oxfam's Research and Evaluation Department*

.

Personal communication in conversation from the following:

Hugh Belshaw, Peter Crichton, Nick Gardner, Sashi Rajangopalan, Patrick Sweeting, Gaby Taylor, Barry Underwood.

Appendix

IDENTIFYING RURAL FINANCIAL NEEDS

1. Approaching rural communities

The purpose of this appendix is to put forward a framework for use by development workers seeking to discover what possible needs exist for savings and/or the provision of credit which are not being met by existing institutions in rural communities.

The first task in attempting to understand a community's financial institutions and needs is to learn about its general social and economic structure, not only about the way in which its members use savings and credit. The next few pages focus on the types of questions that may be asked in order to gain such an understanding. Four suggested checklists of questions are given which could act as guides in informal conversations in villages. This provides a cheaper and quicker means of obtaining information than through more traditional and extensive statistical surveys.

Experience shows the importance of participation in devising credit programmes (see Chapter 8) and how crucial it is to involve members of poor households, especially women, and not just male household heads. The questions to be asked fall under two main headings, reflecting the features which must be understood in order to identify rural financial needs.

2. Household economic relationships and use of savings and credit

Once the internal economic system of a household is understood, the way it makes use of credit can be more accurately estimated. Checklist 1 provides a framework for investigating this internal economic system. It consists of a list of household activities, for each of which the household decision-maker, and the way in which any income it generates is disposed of within the household, need to be determined. It should be possible to identify:

A The range of a household's economic activities – whether many or few, agricultural or non-agricultural, etc.

B The extent to which there are clear divisions of function, particularly according to sex, between household members.

C. The extent to which economic activity and decision-making are fragmented among individuals or groups within the household.

Investigation is likely to reveal quite a wide range of differences between communities in the way in which economic activity is organised.

When the main household unit is an extended family, living together in a 'compound' of as many as 30 or 40 people, economic activity and decision-making tend to be separated. Women may carry out many economic activities largely independently of the rest of the household.
By contrast, where households consist of the three-generation family (children, parents, grandparents), the unit is smaller and more cohesive. Economic activity and decision-making will tend to be 'centralised', although even here there are likely to be some specific jobs which are considered 'women's work' (e.g. weeding and crop processing). Individual family members are likely to carry out some activities independently; for example, the household head may be responsible for house repairs (and therefore for getting the money or materials for them), while women and the elderly may gather forest products or make handicrafts. If the products of these activities are sold, rather than contributed to the household stock, the income earned may be at the disposal of individual members.
While Checklist 1 deals with household economic activities and the income from them, Checklist 2 covers major items of expenditure and the extent to which they are financed by savings and/or credit. The two checklists together provide the means to translate the tree diagram of Chapter 1 into a specific picture of an individual household's main items of expenditure and sources of income (including savings and credit).
The format of Checklist 2 suggests that household members should be asked to recall when major expenditures were made, who made them and what, if any, forms of savings, credit or other income (gifts, state

grants, etc) were used. The data, collected from a representative sample of the community, should give an impression of:

The main types of credit and savings institution used by the community.

The adequacy or otherwise of household savings to meet unusual or large expenditures.

The relative importance of different formal and informal sources of credit.

The main purposes for which credit is used: e.g.
  – day to day consumption needs
  – less frequently occurring consumption
  – investment.

This information ought also to indicate the extent of regular or perpetual indebtedness, and whether the conditions on which loans are made cause borrowers serious distress.

There are wide variations between communities. Some – probably those with a low population and those that are firmly subsistence based – make relatively little use of credit, with households relying mainly on savings to make investments and to meet any unusually high demands for consumption expenditure. Where loans are needed villagers often borrow from relatives or friends rather than traders or moneylenders with whom they lack close links.

In other types of communities, informal credit may be a way of life, with households finding every year that there is a period before harvest when food stocks are exhausted and borrowing is necessary in order to buy food and other necessities, perhaps against the security of a standing crop. When planting time comes, because income from the previous season's crops has all been used up on immediate consumption needs and on repaying past loans, further borrowing is necessary to buy inputs like fertiliser.

Communities in which some households are in this kind of debt cycle are likely to be characterised by inequalities of income and wealth between members. The needs of poor members make them dependent on the wealthier ones, and inequality is reinforced because the wealthy gain resources from the poor as their assets are sold to meet repayment deadlines, or mortgaged crops are valued at below their market price.

Different savings and credit patterns imply that households have different needs. It is therefore necessary to take into account the way in which the structure and institutions of the community as a whole, as distinct from those of the individual household, determine the patterns of existing savings and credit arrangements, and how these will be affected by any new institutions which may be introduced.

3. Community structure and institutions

Exploring the institutions of a community, and the interrelationships between households is more difficult than investigating household economic relationships. Inequality of wealth and power is a sensitive issue, particularly for the wealthy and powerful, and it is often difficult to perceive from outside a community the extent of inequality and its impact on the poor.

Two more checklists, numbers 3 and 4, are suggested for investigating how household decisions are affected by the institutions of the community and by inter-household relations; they can be used as a guide in conversations with the heads and members of a cross-section of households of different wealth and social status.

Checklist 3 consists of a set of questions about the likely constraints on an individual adopting an innovation or making an investment. It is suggested that a specific example be chosen for purposes of discussion in the village. Answers to the questions should indicate the ability or freedom an individual household has to adopt an innovation, and the extent to which it may have to take into account its relationships with other households and to the community as a whole.

Checklist 4 enquires into inter-household relationships in four types of transaction – those relating to the use of land, to the use of labour, to the disposal of produce and to the borrowing/lending of money. The answers should reveal the frequency with which each household engages in each type of transaction, and also provide other indications as to the economic strength or weakness of a household and the extent to which a household's relationships are concentrated or dispersed.

In developed countries economic relationships tend to be contractual and for specific purposes. In villages in the developing world, by contrast, involvement is more complicated, and most people are unwilling or unable to act in ways which cause disapproval from other villagers. Checklist 3 attempts to find out the nature and extent of this; from the answers to it and to Checklist 4, various types of constraints may be revealed.

These may include inequality of power, mutual dependence and a multiplicity in which two people have a complex of relationships often characterized by both inequality and mutual dependence. All these different types of community relationships impose narrow limits on a farmer's scope for decision-making; it is a mistake to assume that it is innate conservatism which restrains the farmer from adopting promising innovations. A farmer in a patron-client relationship will be reluctant to undertake a new activity or join a new group which displeases the patron, while patrons for their part will be suspicious of anything which could reduce a client's dependence.

Poor farmers who are dominated by wealthier neighbours may apparently be at liberty to form a savings group in order to free themselves from loans from landlords or moneylenders, but this may provoke opposition from anyone who stands to lose from such a move. Sanctions, perhaps the withholding of employment, may be applied to dissuade them. In relatively egalitarian societies, where relations of mutual dependence extend widely throughout the community, it may be difficult for one household to adopt any kind of change without repercussions throughout the community.

Land may be cleared for planting annual food crops by communal labour, for example, and a household which fails to participate fully in this because it wants to plant relatively little of a food crop and more of a cash crop, may be seen by others to be neglecting its obligations. Where land is not held under individual title, several households sharing a common ancestor may have a claim to the use of a particular piece of it, and any one of these households may be prevented by the others from doing anything, such as planting trees, which would restrict the use of the plot.

It is easier to obtain agreement for a particular type of change within a group of half-a-dozen households than it is within a village of 50 or 100, especially if they have close links among themselves, but weaker links with the wider community. Smaller household groups with ties of this kind may form the most suitable basis on which to introduce technical or institutional innovations.

4. Intervening in rural financial markets: the choice of options

An investigation of the issues covered in the Appendix reveals the complexity of economic and social relations within the community, including the possible use of institutions both informal (e.g. traders and moneylenders) and formal (e.g. banks). It should then be possible to determine the financial needs of the community, and the ways in which they may be satisfied, using the sort of methodology described in the flow chart in Figure 2.

The left hand column in Figure 2 sets out questions designed to determine the sources of finance potentially available at present; the right hand column indicates forms of intervention which may be possible and appropriate at each stage. There are clearly situations in which households do not need outside help to gain access to credit. They may have the capacity to accumulate the funds they need within their communities, in which case it may be appropriate to encourage savings groups, possibly by adapting indigenous institutions, (taking care not to do more harm than good).

Although even poor households can demonstrate considerable savings capacity, saving is nearly impossible where there is chronic or perpetual indebtedness; households may then need a 'liberation loan', perhaps in the form of credit on reasonable terms from a revolving loan fund. Oxfam's experience is that there is considerable scope for helping small borrowers gain access to formal sources of credit; an agency's role can often lie in encouraging group formation and in acting as an intermediary in negotiations with the lender. Only relatively rarely should agency funds be committed directly to a long-term lending programme.

The main stages in this approach are as follows:

1. Explore and identify financial needs first, before considering the resources which might be used to meet them.

2. Where poor access to suitable finance prevents these needs being met, investigate the scope for mobilising the community's own resources.

3. Where indigenous resources are clearly inadequate, explore and encourage the use of appropriate external financial markets.

4. Only consider committing agency funds to a credit programme where these markets are unable to meet the specific need identified.

5. Aim to reduce, and eventually eliminate, the commitment of agency funds (by the approach outlined in 2 and 3 above), as quickly as possible, and never allow it to become permanent or semi-permanent.

Figure 2 A flow chart approach to meeting rural financial needs

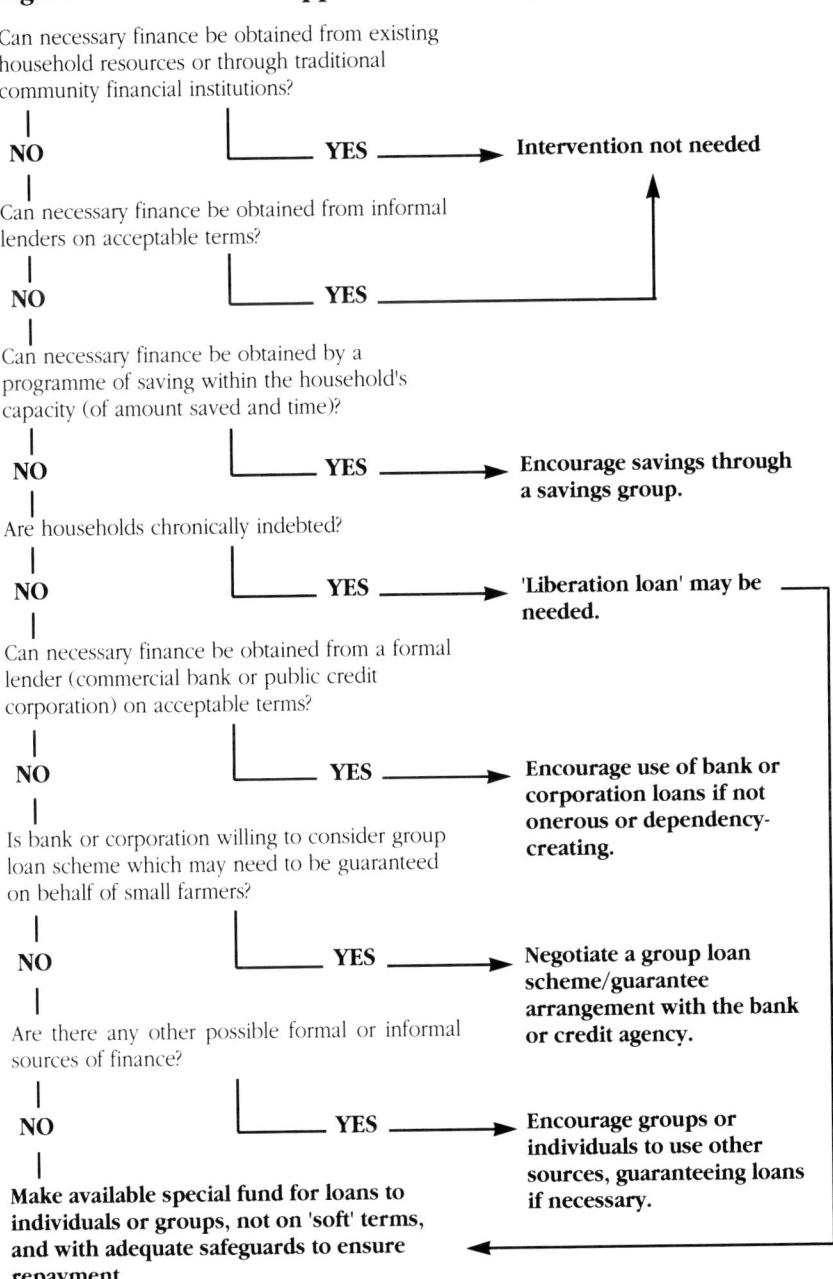

Can necessary finance be obtained from existing household resources or through traditional community financial institutions?

NO

YES ⟶ **Intervention not needed**

Can necessary finance be obtained from informal lenders on acceptable terms?

NO

YES

Can necessary finance be obtained by a programme of saving within the household's capacity (of amount saved and time)?

NO

YES ⟶ **Encourage savings through a savings group.**

Are households chronically indebted?

NO

YES ⟶ **'Liberation loan' may be needed.**

Can necessary finance be obtained from a formal lender (commercial bank or public credit corporation) on acceptable terms?

NO

YES ⟶ **Encourage use of bank or corporation loans if not onerous or dependency-creating.**

Is bank or corporation willing to consider group loan scheme which may need to be guaranteed on behalf of small farmers?

NO

YES ⟶ **Negotiate a group loan scheme/guarantee arrangement with the bank or credit agency.**

Are there any other possible formal or informal sources of finance?

NO

YES ⟶ **Encourage groups or individuals to use other sources, guaranteeing loans if necessary.**

Make available special fund for loans to individuals or groups, not on 'soft' terms, and with adequate safeguards to ensure repayment.

Checklist 1

Productive household activities and division of function between household members

(Single tick for "works on activity"; double tick for "makes decision")

Activity	Head	Wife	Eldest Son	Other
			Household Member	
Cultivating crops for household consumption				
Cultivating crops for sale				
Raising livestock/milking				
Gathering food/fishing/hunting				
Transporting produce				
Marketing produce				
Processing produce for sale/storage				
Storing/taking care of produce				
Maintaining farming equipment, including irrigation works				
Cooking for the family				
Making clothes for the family				
Fetching water for drinking				
Gathering firewood				
Housebuilding and maintenance				
Making household goods – pots, mats, etc.				
Making goods for sale e.g. weaving				
Providing services for sale e.g. haircutting, schooling				
Trading in goods				
Collecting manure				
Wage labour elsewhere				
Child care				
List other activities here:				

Checklist 2

Major household expenditure and use of savings and credit.

Occasions	Household Member	Source of savings and credit (if any)
Buying tin for roof	Household head	Selling gold, borrowing from trader who supplies tin
Paying bride price	Son	Selling goats, borrowing from friends
Buying daughter's marriage gifts	Wife	Contributions from a rotating savings club
Buying food after harvest failure	Household head	Borrowing from relatives, borrowing from village head

Checklist 3

Community constraints on adoption of an innovation

1. Does the farmer require permission (or approval) of a village leader before undertaking the new activity?

2. Does s/he have obligations to share money paid to him/her, or his/her income?
e.g. – a share of the crop to the landlord
    – a tribute to the village head or religious leader
    – an obligation to pool his or her funds with a group

3. Is s/he involved in any communal labour which limits the farming activities s/he can undertake?
e.g. – communal land clearing
    – harvesting
    – irrigation works building

4. Does the new agricultural activity being considered affect others?
e.g. – by using up scarce water
    – by increasing the risk of pests or fire
    – by poisoning with insecticides
    – by overshadowing neighbours' crops
    – by causing deterioration in the village's stock of land

5. Does the household's place in the community limit the sorts of activity it is expected to undertake?
e.g. – due to caste
    – due to tribal background
    – due to head of household's age

6. Are there rules concerning buying and selling land or land use which will affect the farmer?

7. Does the village contain established political groupings which might restrict those who could benefit from a new policy?

8. Would the success of the farmer result in other village members becoming worse off as a result of his/her having access to more of a scarce resource?
e.g. – land
    – water
    – manure

Checklist 4

Types of inter-household transaction

Does the household carry out any of the following	With many house-holds	With few house-holds	With none at all	Notes
1.1 Lease out land				
1.2 Share use of land with other households				
1.3 Rent land				
1.4 Share-crop land				
2.1 Employ labour				
2.2 Exchange labour				
2.3 Sell its labour				
2.4 Work to pay off debts or similar commitments				
3.1 Sell farm produce for cash				
3.2 Buy produce from others for re-sale				
3.3 Sell produce before harvest for cash				
3.4 Deliver produce in repayment of debt				
4.1 Lend money at interest				
4.2 Make interest-free loans				
4.3 Participate in reciprocal savings/ credit arrangement				
4.4 Borrow from relatives				
4.5 Borrow from landlord				
4.6 Borrow from other wealthy villagers				